Alcester
My Early Days

*Dedicated to my family and friends who have
been the driving force behind this book.*

*Front cover top: Alcester High Street in the 1950s.
Front cover bottom: Alcester High Street, Alcester Cadets bringing home
the cups. Rear cover top: Alcester High Street, 2017. Rear cover middle:
Marian Trout, Winnie Biddle and Eric Payne tidying up the small
entrance to the church. Rear cover bottom: Alcester Town Hall, 2017.*

*Picture credits: p10, p15, p70, rear cover top & rear cover bottom
courtesy of Alistair Brewin, p18 courtesy of David Malin.*

Alcester
My Early Days

"Louise"

Maggie Payne

Maggie Payne

BREWIN BOOKS

First published by
Brewin Books Ltd, 56 Alcester Road,
Studley, Warwickshire B80 7LG in 2017
www.brewinbooks.com

ISBN: 978-1-85858-574-1

A Cataloguing in Publication Record
for this title is available from the British Library.

Typeset in Haarlemmer MT Std
Printed in Great Britain by
Hobbs The Printers Ltd.

CONTENTS

INTRODUCTION

We can talk of the 'old days' in our home town wherever we live, but it's sometimes better to put it down on paper when imagining or remembering these special places and how life used to be.

Here I write about the shops, some of the characters and the way of life in the 50s and 60s in a little town called Alcester. These vivid memories stay in my mind, and I hope they will bring back memories for the reader too.

Shops and offices change but the characters are still to be found if you look for them.

Money was not always there or even facilities.

No! Life was more simple then. Shop premises didn't have electronic tills, but a notebook and pen ready to add large items up if it were too complicated for the brain to work out. Some type of uniform was worn to determine who worked in which shop.

Children were free to go anywhere without fear.

Policemen were regularly seen appearing round any corner at any time of the day or night, and to be feared.

FOOD AND CLEANLINESS

Coming home from school we were always hungry but not allowed anything luxurious as there was never anything to be found in the pantry. We were allowed, however, to share a tomato sauce sandwich, or just a sugar sandwich before the evening meal. On a good day it was sliced banana sandwiches with sugar sprinkled on.

Occasionally I would watch my mother skinning a rabbit, never flinching, ready to eat the next day. Sometimes as a treat she would ask what I would like for tea another day. I always asked for lambs' hearts! Would I eat either now? NO!

Thankfully some of the old recipes for food still thrive, rice pudding, fruit pies, and steamed puddings.

Kippers were always a treat to have for breakfast. On cold winter nights we would take it in turn to toast pikelets on a long iron fork over the blazing fire, afterwards playing cards, dominoes, reading books or learning to knit. We were never allowed to play cards on a Sunday as it was the Sabbath.

The ashes from the previous night were shovelled up and put into the metal dustbin. Needless to say the vacuum was out more times than in due to the dust from the ashes. Tins of Johnsons polish were always to be seen in every household where all wooden furniture was highly polished. Many homes had tins of Red Cardinal polish to brighten their stone steps up too. Brasso came out weekly to polish the door knockers or key holes.

Most grocery lists included Persil washing powder, a bag of blue for the whites, Harpic for the toilet and Izal toilet rolls. Let's not forget the scrubbing brush to clean the tiled floors. Tins of Vim or Ajax were a must to keep under the kitchen sink.

Mondays were always wash days. The boiler was on the go most of the day, with the old mangle ready to put the sheets through. Steam filled the kitchen making the windows mist up.

Friday night, as a very young child, was when the old grey tin tub came out where some of us had to bath. My mother would top up the water as I never wanted to get out of it into a cold kitchen. Not always convenient when older brothers would walk in and your hair was soaked in Amami shampoo.

On special occasions such as weddings one of my sisters-in-law would come and 'set' my hair, leaving the rollers in when I went to bed. How did I ever sleep? The torment of those spikes sticking in my head, yet the excitement of the next day to come.

Weddings were always a special occasion, especially when they happened in the road we lived in. A collection went round from house to house to give to the happy couple. Residents would crowd outside the house to see the bride on her way to the church. We were all a kind of family that were always there to support each other in good times or bad.

OVERSLEY HOUSE

Where I lived in the old Roman town of Alcester stood a vast grey building known as Alcester Hospital. This had been the Workhouse or the Poor House for many years until it became a hospital for the aged and infirm. I remember it as Alcester Hospital. Patients, mainly older ones, were brought there when very ill. A huge chimney stood over the hospital blowing soot across the residents washing on a breezy day. Neighbours could be seen rushing out to get the washing in at the same time cursing the black soot that had blown onto the sheets.

A gentleman called Les King was often seen by the tall chimney that overlooked the houses working at 'stoking up'. Les would take time out and stride into town with his trolley, cigarette hanging from his mouth, and plenty of stubble round his chin introducing himself to the locals. A little man with a resounding voice.

From my bedroom window I would see nurses occasionally, hastily running down the lane next to the hospital looking for a patient that had 'got out' and would be found wandering around the town.

The old oak tree dominated the small car park to the front of the hospital. During the autumn, as children, we waited until the conkers were dropping and would spend as much time as we could collecting them ready

Oversley House today.

to have Conker Tournaments in town. This was fine as long as the Matron didn't see you! She was a very smart lady in a crisp, sky blue uniform and starched pure white frilled cap on her head. If she caught sight of us, she would come rushing out of the hospital, clapping her hands shouting 'You have no right here, this is private land!' Of course we would run away, only to go back again when she wasn't around. A small group of us were often in that area and as we got older, we would explore the maze of paths leading to all the wards and peering through Oversley House hospital windows where we were frightened out of our wits on seeing all these elderly people, mostly asleep in pure white bed linen, matching their pure white faces in rows of hospital beds. They all seemed to look the same! The wards seemed so silent.

A friend of mine, Cynthia, told me her mother was an auxiliary nurse and worked nights for about £1 a night. She can remember that there was a balcony at the back of the hospital which she could see from her back garden and if there had been a death during the night the mattress was hung out to air. As she was not very old she could only remember going to see her mother at work, where she would go and talk to the old ladies on the ward. She particularly remembered befriending an old lady called Mrs Bayliss who knitted her a blanket out of squares.

Sometimes we would see the nurses returning from their day's work talking of their experiences during the day. Everyone held these ladies in the highest regard. They themselves had to go home and look after their own families at the end of the day.

Sylvia (Sreeves) told me what the working day consisted of in the hospital. There was a coal fire in the middle of the upstairs ward, the nurses carried the coal upstairs, making sure the ward was always kept warm. In those days the nurses acted as hairdressers and chiropodists as well as nursing the patients.

The air raid shelter was used as the mortuary, where the nurses always put flowers to make it a more pleasant surrounding. When it was a full moon, one lady would cover her head so only her eyes were revealed. For what reason, no one ever knew! Maybe some hidden torment trying to get out.

There was fun to be found at the right time. Sylvia was known to dress up in men's long pants and dress in 'fun' clothes to entertain the residents. That was until she heard the Matron coming, when she immediately had to hide. The Matron at the time, was very efficient, but very fair.

All of the nurses lived close by so were in easy reach to go to work. Here are just a few: Sister Crootes, Winnie Smith, Mollie Smith, Cissie Dyke, Phyliss Delaney, Jill Holmes, Brenda Dexter, Helen Woodfield, Ivy Hall, Frank Woodfield (Gardener), Nellie Fitzgerald, Mollie Morgan, Yvonne Wootton, Fred Tarver (Porter), Barbara Kirpitchinock, Mrs Schofield and Mary Butler.

Most of the patients were sent to Alcester Hospital by the local Doctors. One such gentleman was Dr Fitzpatrick, living in Kinwarton Road by the river. 'Dr Fitz' as he was known would greet mothers with their children sitting at his desk, with 'Now then Mrs, what's up with her?' Very down to earth was Dr Fitz, puffing and panting from the daily cigarettes he smoked. And the aroma of whisky, I guess for his own medicinal purposes. On his rounds visiting patients, the child would have to be downstairs as the Doctor found it difficult climbing stairs to bedrooms due to him being out of breathe. He had occasion to visit us when my mother called him out to my brother David. My mother had seven children to look after, and on this particular time it was David who was diagnosed with tonsillitis, they would have to be removed at the local hospital. At the same time my other brother Norman was screaming the place down so Dr Fitz inquired as to what was the matter with him? Mother replied 'nothing he's just crying for attention'. Sadly for Norman, the Doctor took one look at him and said 'take him to the hospital with his brother and he can have his 'b—gg—s out as well'!

My youngest brother Phillip was informed by Dr Fitz that he had to wear spectacles at a young age. Being the stubborn one that he was, he decided he didn't like them so flushed them down the toilet. Suffice to say he went many years without wearing any at all, but coped very well.

All this was in the days when the Doctor never seemed to have a day off, except for one Sunday. Coming out of Sunday school I was chasing a friend when I slipped up a kerb cutting my knee open quite badly. Blood was pouring out profusely so I was taken into the Baptist Chapel nearby where the local nurse (Mrs Clarke) lived close by in the cottages called Malt Mill Lane. She tried hard to stop the bleeding but without success so she advised my mother to take me straight to the Doctor where upon we were greeted by what was known as his nurse/housekeeper. She told us he couldn't see anyone at this time and that she would bandage my knee as best she could until the next morning. The following day, we went back to the surgery only to be told by the Doctor that the said knee should have been stitched. My mother immediately bounced back saying 'It would have been if you had bothered to come out from your afternoon nap yesterday!' Dr Fitz did like his whisky!

I was bandaged up and after several weeks the knee mended leaving a hole where it should have been knitted together.

Almost opposite the Doctor's was a corner shop known as 'Rimells' where Bill and Sally Bayley now live. Such a tiny shop which sold grocery, confectionery etc. It was the first shop nearest the town to visit if time was short. The children would love to put their money in the chewing gum machine against the wall outside and get a packet of Wrigley's Spearmint out, but only after school and if you could afford it, or even if you were allowed to eat such 'rubbish' as my mother told me.

Like many shops the dwelling quarters were attached. Such tiny places but what were called 'home'.

SPRING GARDENS

Opposite the corner shop were a row of cottages known as 'Spring Gardens'. What a lovely name! Mrs Chatterley lived in one of these cottages with her family and the famous Bant Richardson. 'Bant' as he was known, looked after the local orchard about 100 yards away. Where now a shopping precinct stands, rows and rows of apple trees, fruit bushes, and strawberries could be found. Each day would be taken up with Bant chasing the youngsters away after they were caught stealing the fruit or climbing the trees. A wall surrounded the tiny cottages where Bant lived. During the summer months he would display baskets of strawberries to sell to passers by.

Mrs Cole (Maggie) known as Granny Cole, also lived in Spring Gardens. She had black hair and was always smiling. Granny Cole was a very smart lady, wearing a black hat with a feather rose in it. Inside her cottage was a large brass fender which could be sat on. Beside this was a large curved kettle.

Each evening she would go to The Red Horse public house just down the road, carrying her enamel jug to put her favourite beer in. Her profession was the local fortune teller whose door was always open for anyone wanting to know what the future had in store for them. She had two crystal balls but would never tell her family their fortunes as it was said to be unlucky. The children were told to go upstairs while Granny Cole attended to business when visitors came. The 'real' crystal ball she kept in a bright red velvet bag, the second one was kept in her top drawer.

Living right next to the river flowing under Gunnings Bridge, the cottages were always being flooded out. It was the norm for the residents, children were told 'it will be gone tomorrow' and so it was.

Bottom of School Road, Spring Gardens to the right (now demolished).

Granny Cole would walk to Redditch, some miles away to sell pegs from a wooden basket. Word has it there was French blood in her family and she was related to Maurice Chevalier! Maggie Cole died in her late 80s and is buried with her husband in Alcester Cemetery.

Gunnings Bridge wall close by, over the river Arrow, is still there today. If you look when passing, you will see indentations where schoolchildren walked along the wall being most careful not to fall into the allotment on the other side. The allotment was kept in perfect condition by Mr Bradley, a very friendly man who always had time for a wave or a chat.

The children who played over the other side of Gunnings Bridge after school or during the holidays, were told to be back home from wherever they were by 4.30pm, before the black and white Maudslay buses came tearing down the hill. They carried men and women who had been at work all day at Rockwell Maudslay in Great Alne, a little village two miles away. So many Alcester people worked in this massive building.

They would catch the buses early in the morning and return the same way at 5 o'clock, the men mostly carrying haversacks on their back and looking tired and weary. There must have been eight black and white coaches all arriving together and dropping the workers off at the bottom of the hill known as Captains Hill. This great firm is where they built parts for the motor industry that went all over the world.

GAS HOUSE LANE

Obviously named as it was where the gas works were. Many children could be seen pushing prams or wheelbarrows along the lane to put coke in to take home for the family's fire in the 50s.

THE GREIG MEMORIAL HALL

In the centre of Kinwarton Road and Gunnings Road The Greig Memorial Hall was erected which was to be the heart of the town for many years after. The main building was built in 1958, with finances supplied by Mr David Greig, a respected and successful businessman, who ran a chain of grocery stores. His wife, Hannah Susan, committed herself to working tirelessly for the youth of Alcester and when she died her husband built the hall in her memory.

The Greig Memorial Hall today.

Most evenings were taken up by the many organisations in the town relating to the youth. This was a God-send for parents as The Hannah Susan Greig Memorial Hall was a reputable place for the youngsters to go to. Church Fellowship evenings on a Tuesday night (run by Mrs Jean Steed) was more of a Youth Club. The Alcester Junior Drama used it every Thursday to rehearse pantomimes for the New Year. The performance consisted of Friday evening, Saturday afternoon Matinee and Saturday evening. There were many concerts and variety shows held regularly, each time tickets were sold out before the performance.

A great variety of evening classes were held there, in fact every room was used frequently. In later years, the Hall was utilised for Concerts, Dinners, Weddings, Dances, Fetes, Carnivals and Horticultural Shows. You name it!

Managers such as David Pick were there to greet you at the door, respectably dressed in a dark suit, crisp white shirt and polished shoes, to assist in any way. A beautiful, well-kept and maintained building, the premises consisted of a large main hall including a bar. The perfect stage for the annual Pantomime, with blue velvet curtains and dressing rooms at the

Alcester Junior Drama Amateur Dramatics Group at The Greig Memorial Hall.

back for the ladies and gents, complete with toilets. The joys of growing up in your mid teens in Alcester. Although young men were on one side in the back rooms and young girls the other side during performances, there were still interesting goings on in-between acts in the back rooms and down the concrete stairs leading up to the stage where the pantomime was being performed on the stage at the time! I'm sure many could tell stories of this glorious building over the years.

A separate room called the Thistle Room is where you would find a smaller bar. The kitchen was meticulously clean. The toilets and cloak room had an attendant to help you and look after your coat. To the side was what was known as the Green Room where Committee meetings were held. In the foyer the marble statue of The Greig Family stood on a highly polished marble floor. Every day this magnificent hall was used by one of the organisations in town.

On Friday evenings the local Girl Guides gathered there. During my younger years I had three 'Captains' of the Girl Guides, each devoted to their work. Deirdre Adams, followed by Enid Smith, followed by Wendy Weatherhead. The District Commissioner was Miss Anne Fox. We all knew when this lady was calling in, to be well dressed, smart, polite and ready to answer any questions she may put to us. To gain the badges that we still see today we had to earn them. One very simple task was to use the telephone by ringing the Captain up to show you were able to use the phone. When it was my turn to do it, never being allowed to use the phone at home, I was so nervous I never slept all night! Plucking up courage I dialled the number and meekly said 'Hello Captain Adams, this is Margaret from the Girl Guides ringing you to pass my test'. The reply was short and sweet... 'You have passed your test dear' and she put the phone down! All that worrying for nothing, just a short sweet reply.

We were encouraged to attend Civic services but not before continuously practising marching. Up and down we would stride out in the large main hall, week after week until we got it right. We were all threatened we were there to represent the town and no one wanted to see sloppy walking! Uniforms were inspected beforehand and no coats were allowed to be worn, no matter how

A party at The Greig Memorial Hall during the 1960s.

cold. I'm sure most girls will remember the camp fire nights. All such sweet innocent memories before actually growing up.

Sadly the building closed down in the 1990s, no longer could the community gather in this beautiful building, and now at the time of writing The Greig Memorial Hall awaits confirmation of its future.

ALCESTER TOWN FOOTBALL CLUB

Hidden away by the recreational ground at the other end of town was a wooden hut, mainly used by football teams every Saturday. Showers were fitted in and, as a young girl, I was fascinated to see the footballers going in smelling of embrocation (obviously the door was closed!) but coming out looking like gentlemen and smelling of the latest aftershave.

Football matches were held every Saturday in Stratford Road. An unbelievable 'event' happened one Saturday when we were laughing at the cows in the next field, wired off, being so close. We jokingly said what would happen if they jumped the fence? THEY DID! I've never seen so many footballers run away and clear the field!

Many times there was an away match. One particular day we arrived at Feckenham where the heavens opened with a torrential thunder storm making it impossible to play this important match. Food was already laid on so the only thing to do was to stop in the pub. This was mid afternoon. We left about midnight with many happy faces. This would never happen today since the drink driving law came out.

The club building also had other uses. Many Country and Western nights were held there, with a licensed bar. The 'bouncer' was Roger Floyd who was there to deter anyone wanting to cause trouble. Sadly Roger was caught in the cross fire one night after he fought off youths who wanted to cause mischief. The next day he was seen with a battered and bruised face, eyes nearly closed and black and blue. It didn't deter him; again he was there every time there was a function but thankfully there was no more trouble.

Every Monday evening the room was packed with locals for the weekly Bingo. Of course the regulars were there early to book their seats and woe betide any new person who sat in them! Eric Payne was the caller and came out with many innuendos! There was always a throw back from one or two of the customers. Eric used to say these senior ladies made him blush… but he did ask for it! Those who won could be meek and mild calling out 'bingo' if they had won and then there were those who shouted for Alcester! 'BINGO'! Elsie Mills comes to mind. All for the wonderful sum of £2 or £3 depending on how many turned up on the night.

THE NATIONAL SCHOOL

Moving down into School Road was the National School with its very old building sitting right next to the old cemetery.

In the winter, children would walk from wherever they lived in thick coats, long socks, gloves or mittens and often sit through the day in the same clothes if the heating had broken down. Milk would arrive in small glass bottles, children would then receive the drinking straw only to find out that it was impossible to consume as the milk was still frozen! In the summer the milk had been left out in the sun and was often too warm to drink.

A 1950s school photo. Back Row: Ray Moore, Eileen Gooding, Jill Davies, Margaret Price, Eleanor Butler, Jennifer Dyke, Ann Sutor, Eileen Sallis, Maureen Mertens, Barbara Headley, Les Savage. Middle Row: Miss Elsie Skinner, Jill Gardener, David Coles, Brian Cresswell, David Smith, John Smith, George Hall, Frankie Priest, Michael Burden, Beryl Cornish. Third Row: Eileen Ward, Mary Blundell, Christine Smith, June Isles, Mary Docker, Terry Vernon, Melvyn Stevens, Wallace Read, Fred Bates. Bottom Row left: David Hemming, Roy Beesley, Brian Edge, Eric Payne, Hughie Green, Johnny Maxfield, Ray Chatterley.

It was always a joy for any child to see snow at the weekend. The favourite place to go was Primrose Hill in Oversley. Some children had well-built, home-made sledges, others used plastic containers. Children could be seen pulling each other along the roads outside their homes and snow balling.

Most children stayed at school all day and had their dinner across the road in a hut, known as The Youth Hut. This was next to a large field used by the school for sports and summer fetes. On entering the hut, we would line up to have our dinner served by the kitchen staff, three of whom were

Children playing in the snow at the top of Malt Mill Lane.

Mrs Careless, Mrs Simmons and Mrs Doris Fletcher. You didn't get a choice as to what you wanted, it was all just put on your plate.

In this same hut, lessons were also taught, usually by Mrs Bretherton. She was a tall and elegant lady who was very nice but stood no nonsense. We were introduced to needlework and in one lesson a little girl kept 'back chatting' above Mrs Bretherton's voice. The teacher did no more than call the girl to her desk where she promptly gave her a good hiding and told she would never answer back again in her classroom. Nor did she!

Every Christmas, as with many schools, the children displayed their talents with a small concert. Many were chosen to be fairies which meant parents had to find the material to make their little darlings look angelic. Material was bought from nearby Redditch Open Market, brought home and the costume made either by your mother or a near neighbour who was a good seamstress.

The toilets in the school remained the same for many years. Very tiny with wooden seats. They never seemed hygienic but when needs must who cares! A gentleman called Mr Saul was the caretaker, always seen around the school with either a wheelbarrow or a sweeping brush in his hand. He was a tall man always friendly to the children and stopping to chat. Mr Jenkins was the headmaster but left some time in the 50s when Mr and Mrs Wilson came along during the mid 50s. The headmaster lived in the School House which was on the premises. As I remember the teachers were: Mrs Parkes, Mrs Bretherton, Mr Grinnell, Miss Skinner, Miss Balmforth, Mr Silver, Mrs Wilson, Miss Hamelin, Mr Williams, Mr Thomas and Mrs McAllister (this lady I remember so vividly with bright ginger hair). She put the fear of God in me at the infants school when she announced, if I didn't get a particular sum right, I would be banned from the school. Funny how you remember these things! Would it happen today to a 7-year-old?

There were approximately 36 children to a class with the occasional 'student' to help out. Trips out were to Oversley farm, two miles away, to visit the cows and sheep.

To the right of School Road in Alcester was a large cemetery. As children we would walk rather quickly going past this area as it always seemed a sad place. The old Alms Houses next door with their huge shrubs of lavender were a welcome sight and smell after passing the cemetery. Next door stood Alcester Grammar School, built in the last century.

Children were seen daily walking or biking home from school in smart blazers, red and black ties, boys wearing caps and the girls straw boaters. Only a certain amount of children (about five or six) ever passed the 11 plus exam from the junior school to go to the Grammar School as it was a much smaller school in the 50s. That's my excuse for not passing.

A new Junior School was built in St Faiths Road. This was known as St Faiths C of E School taking in children for the 11 plus exam. Every morning we would have assembly in the main hall where Mr Wilson who also moved there, always ended with the same prayer:

Lighten our darkness, we beseech thee, O Lord; and by thy great mercy defend us from all perils and dangers of this night; for the love of thy only Son, our Saviour Jesus Christ. *Amen.*

As children we often wondered what was going to happen in the evening after that prayer!

As the first people to use this school it was a real treat! Bright and sparkling, very modern with lovely windows looking out onto the open fields at the back. Toilets with actual sinks and a drinking fountain to use at anytime. The front of the building leading up to the school was a nightmare for parents as the roads had not been finished so was just black rubble and dirt. Clean socks ended up very dirty on returning home after school. A massive 'hill', as we called it, consisting of dry mud dominated the entrance to the school as work wasn't quite finished outside, this was a haven for the children to jump or climb during play time. The school had a lovely field for sports day activities. Relays were the favourite when everyone was gunning for the local girls, Jean Currier, Anne Brookes and Wendy Faulkner as they proved to be the best runners. Jean went on to County levels and did very well. She seemed to run like the wind.

Days out were no surprise, it was either London or London Airport. Although exciting, (the thought of a day out!) most children had to go home and explain to their parents how much it would cost! I guess it's the same today! Parents must have dreaded that day wondering how much time they had to save the money up.

The day came when we had to leave this lovely school and prepare to become a senior. Those that didn't pass for the Grammar School were given the choice of Studley High School or Bidford High School. Mr Wilson, came on the last day and wished us well in

Old School teachers. Back row: Joe and Kitty Wilson. Front row: Dorothy Barmforth and Elsie Skinner.

whatever school we went to but advised our true colours would come out by the end of schooling! How right he was!

In 1960 what an eye opener Studley High School was. Many scholars could tell stories of the Headmaster but suffice to say; yes he did use the cane on girls and boys!

Fresh new uniforms were bought (maroon and yellow) to start our new life. Thick striped dresses for the girls in summer. Occasionally the girls were summoned to the main hall and told to kneel on the floor. Along came the Headmistress who would promptly tell those of us with 'sugared' or starched underskirts to take them off and to also roll down from the waist the dress that should be on the knees!

The old buses would arrive at the bottom of the road and would leave dead on 8.30am to take us to school. A lovely lady called Mrs Beaman was put in charge of seeing there was no trouble with the passengers. Being new students we quickly learnt the older scholars always had the back seats and that our turn would come one day to dominate those seats. Often we could smell cigarette smoke coming from the back of the bus, Mrs Beaman would always shout to the boys but never reported them. Happy days!

If asked 'who was your favourite teacher?' I'm sure many would say Mr John Earle, now retired and living in Great Alne, he was the Art and Music teacher. During long hot summer days Mr Earle would take us to sit under a large oak tree on the school field and conduct our Art lessons there instead of a stuffy, hot classroom. The patience he had, he never seemed to raise his voice. This gentleman also formed a choir which everyone was glad to attend. Over and over we would practise and the dear man would say in a high pleasant voice 'got it?'

Biology lessons were not what you thought. We were required to get a bull's eye from the butcher and dissect it. I do not remember what the purpose was!

Morning Assembly was a nightmare. Each class formed rows and were told to stand up straight and sing. Often the school did not please the Headmaster with not reaching the high notes in the hymns. In a resounding voice you would hear him repeatedly shout from the stage 'AGAIN!' If anyone fainted we were told to 'leave them'. What the teachers thought I really don't know! Yes, it was a very strict school.

I loved the cookery lessons and it was the fashion to have gondola baskets but these proved very difficult in carrying the casseroles that we made. My mother was looking forward to cauliflower cheese which we had to make in the cookery lesson, it turned out beautifully. As my mother was at the shops when I returned from school, I left the dish on the floor by the front door. We came to sit down for the evening meal and egg and chips were put in front of us. On inquiring where the cauliflower cheese was my mother said she had returned from the shops only to find a cat eating it! In the bin it went.

Unfortunately, I was sent out of the classroom one morning because I had forgotten to put sugar in the rock cakes I was baking! I had been stood outside for about an hour when I heard the steel heels of the headmaster coming down the corridor. There was nowhere to hide except under the open stairs so I knew I had to face up to whatever was coming. I was marched off to the Headmaster's office. I stood outside for an hour before he called me into his office where he produced a long thin cane! I was told to hold both my hands out, he lifted my hands higher with the cane giving me the riot act on how I should concentrate more. Thankfully the cane slowly came down but not on my hands. I was given 'lines' to do by the next morning consisting of the words 'I must learn to control myself'. My confession also is that I was given lines many times over four years with those exact same words. Were they trying to tell me something? I just got lucky as my friend unfortunately had six of the best on each hand, all because a boy who sat behind her, prodded her in the back with his ruler and she shouted 'OUCH!' so was sent to the Headmaster's office.

Cross Country consisted of running round a large field with sheep dotted about, running around the church and back to the road where we had set off. It was quite possible when teachers weren't looking to run across the front of the church missing a lot of ground out.

On the last day of school, lessons were as normal and P.E. (Physical Education) was held during the afternoon. Unfortunately a small incident

Alcester National School.

happened involving a group of us girls throwing an 'item' of clothing belonging to someone else from a top window. The 'item' was pay back time for a girl who always seemed to get out of P.E. lessons over the years when the weather was scorching hot or the frost was on the ground! Just as the garment went out of the high window, the Headmistress called us with her finger to go down to the office. Of course we had a good telling off, the leaving gift as it was our last day. No more could anyone give us those lines saying 'I must learn to control myself' at least 100 times.

The feeling of freedom was exciting, we were now allowed to live our own lives, or so we thought! This I will recall later on.

TRANSPORT BY TRAIN

We must not forget Station Road and the old Railway Station. The highlight of the weekend was to catch the train as a treat to go shopping in

Birmingham, Evesham or Redditch or to the local Cinema. Just to stand on the platform was a pleasure, watching the trains come and go. Mr Saunders was the Station Master and lived in the little cottage on the premises with his wife and three boys. The garden was kept beautifully with traditional flowers welcoming you to the burgundy coloured doors leading to the ticket office. Lupins and hollyhocks towered over the wooden fence of the Station House as you walked to the station.

On visiting relatives my mother and I would catch the early morning train to Beckford near Tewkesbury and walk two miles through long lanes to reach my Auntie's cottage. On returning my mother would come home laden with knitted goods, home-made jam and marmalade. What a tiresome jaunt it was walking back to the train. All the complaining in the world about legs aching didn't do any good as we had to make it to the train station or be stranded. Relaxing in the train on return for the next 15-20 miles was such a relief, and then we had to walk back home another mile.

Alcester Station.

THE LOCAL TRADERS

On the main Birmingham road, opposite Ragley Mill Lane was a travellers' rest – Alec's Café, a thriving place for many weekend bike riders and lorry drivers to stop. 'Alec' Whiting was a real character and his premises were next to the large factory known as The Cabinet Works, owned by the Ison family, producing furniture items.

Although only a small road, a second big factory also thrived in business at the time. Herbert Terry & Co. had made springs and corset fasteners since 1911. In 1968 Denisons took over making supermarket equipment, and as I recall, clothes airers for the washing along with many inexpensive household goods. Baby Buggies were a great favourite in the town, one touch of a clip and this small contraption fell into an easy thing to carry when getting on buses etc. These were popular as they were light and easy to fold.

Following on to Priory Road four shops were very popular. Mrs Everitt's confectionery shop was a must, especially at the weekends for the ice cream. Mr and Mrs Everitt ran this tiny confectioners shop for years. It was every child's dream to walk in and see Mrs Everitt come through the green living room door and say 'Hello Dear, what would you like today?' She had lots of patience while waiting for children to decide what they would like. The little shop was opposite Alcester's 'Turys', a word not many people outside the town know about. They are little alleys leading from one street to another, saving time in walking all the way around the town. A very welcome short cut.

Mrs Everitt was also the local nurse visiting all the schools around Warwickshire. She was also known as 'the nit nurse'. She regularly visited all the local schools with her white comb and white cloth to put round your neck, and seemed to rake through your hair in the hope of finding those little black midgets. Thankfully most people were clean-headed but you still dreaded the visit. You could get your National Dried Baby milk powder and orange juice for your babies from this lady.

From my own experience in later years, when married, Mrs Everitt's was the shop to call in to buy sweets on our way to six o'clock Evensong church service on Sundays, this was the bribery to keep the children quiet and encourage them to go to church!

Further down the road was yet another confectionery shop which was first run by Mrs Crouch, Mrs Stokes then took over the running of it. During the 60s, Sylvia and Barry Statham worked their together for many years selling the finest ice cream and old fashioned confectionery, always happy in their work. Although a delight to walk into both these shops the dreaded Dentist was in-between the two confectioners, situated in a row of houses known as Hertford House. Mr Gaydon was a man to fear. On passing these houses the smell of the dentist would frequently waft up your nose. Walking into his room, it was so old fashioned with the dreaded seat in the middle. Maybe it was me, but he never seemed gentle once those 'pliers' were in your mouth. Many nights of broken sleep before visiting were a nightmare in themselves. I always wondered why parents gave you a big white handkerchief to use after teeth were extracted. Why a white handkerchief?

At the very end of Priory Road was Mrs Perry's Wool Shop. Although a tiny establishment, you would find a wide variety of yarns, cotton, wool, stockings and knitting pattern books. Regular shoppers would visit and at the same time catch up with the Alcester news. Always a happy shop to call into, Mrs Madge Perry was the proprietor but had regular assistants to help out, her daughter, Mrs Jean James and Mrs Doll Tanner and Tina Bennett. There was always such a wonderful atmosphere on walking in. Each shop had its own smell and yes you could even smell the wool as you walked in the door. Rows and rows of all colours and strengths were piled high from the wooden floor to the ceiling. Small it may have been but trade was good. So many varieties of wool and knitting patterns could be found there. Knitting and crocheting were very fashionable years ago after seeing people such as Twiggy modelling knitted and crocheted items of clothing in the newspapers and magazines.

'Doll' was known to go out and speak to all the new mothers with babies saying how beautiful they all were, hence to encourage the mothers to go inside the shop and buy something.

EVESHAM STREET

Moving round to Evesham Street passing the Globe Hotel (which is mentioned later) we find the Alcester Co-op. This was a large establishment consisting of a Grocery shop and a large Haberdashery store. As children we were fascinated to go in and watch the procedure of the money changing hands. I remember my mother asking to see men's singlets. Singlets? What on earth were they? Of course out from one of the drawers tucked away behind the counter came the men's vests. She would then ask for socks or handkerchiefs, again another drawer would open.

Payment was usually made by a 10 shilling note which was put into a metal contraption with a lid. The assistant, Mrs Steele, would then screw the lid down and within seconds this money container would whizz along a piece of cord above your head to the cashier sat in a little room all of her own at the top of a few stairs. From there the money would be removed and any change put back in and the container whizzed back again to the shop assistant. Now imagine all that performance! I don't suppose they ever had the shop raided as the security of being at a slightly higher level would deter anyone.

Also in the shop were Ladies and Gents clothing, hats, shoes, curtain material and always a well dressed window display. In the early 60s all the girls were desperate to have the blue and white polka dot dress which was in the window of the Co-op. It took me ages to save up for it but at the last moment, worried there would be no more on sale, I went to my father pleading for him to give me the last half crown I needed to get this dress. He gave in gracefully, saying not to tell my mother. Nor did I!

Occasionally the Co-op Insurance man would pop in on his rounds. Mr Ernie Steele (husband of Mrs Steele) was full of laughter and always ready to have a chat.

Evesham Street was very much the Co-op's Street. Opposite was the butchers, run by Jack Salmons and Ray Sutor. Butchers were always in competition with each other but customers who shopped at the Co-op were always loyal to the Co-op and it made sense to shop all in one go.

SWAN STREET

Back in Swan Street was one of the local hairdressers and barbers. Now, for a short back and sides Arthur Keyte's hairdressers was the place to be. To the left were the ladies hairdressers, where the pungent smell of strong perming solution would waft from the door. Often the colour of the ladies' hair would be blue or purple and tightly curled when they walked out. To the right was the gent's hairdressers where the hairdresser was Percy Keyte, Barber Keyte as he was known. As he was cutting young boys' hair he could be heard singing the song 'Underneath the spreading chestnut tree, I saw her, she saw me', why we will never know! A local lady, Alice Sreeves washed all the towels for him for sixpence. Barber Keyte did not charge serving soldiers in the war for their hair cuts.

Opposite Mr Jack Swindlehurst ran a small garage, remembering there were not many cars about in those days.

Bill Sanky, now there's a strange name, he was next door selling and mending bicycles. A fine display could be seen in the showroom as the traffic passed round the Globe Public House into Swan Street.

As a thought, who remembers sweet tobacco, rhubarb custards and coloured raindrops? Such a tiny little sweet shop in Swan Street run by Mrs Westbury, who sold all these delights. As you entered the shop, a bell rang and out would come Mrs Westbury from her little living room, always dressed in long brown skirts or dresses, brown lace up shoes with a cube heel, brown hair and her brown, round glasses halfway down her nose. Thinking about it, the little shop was painted brown as well! Maybe it was the 'in' colour!

Whilst we looked for what we could get for three pence, she would be getting out the small triangular white bag and meticulously weighing a quarter of an ounce of whatever was chosen on the oval shaped weighing scales.

Swan Street was a short road and seemed very quiet. Maybe that's why the library was there, obviously a peaceful place. Notices read SILENCE when you walked in the door. A lovely lady would be stood behind the counter, ready to mark the books. In a way it was always an adventure to see so many books… and always one just waiting for you. The clue in finding the right book was to see how many others had read it. If say just three readers had been stamped on the inside of the book, then I'd put it back on the shelf and look for another which had been stamped many times. This way I knew it was a popular book.

Fridays and Saturdays, whilst walking in Swan Street around lunch time, there would be the heavenly smell of fish and chips. Bill Devey could be seen in his white apron slamming the potatoes through the chip slicer and doing an excellent trade, the queue was always outside the door. If not at Bill Devey's you would get them at Hutton's fish and chip shop in the High Street. Saturday evenings, people would come out of the local cinema in the High Street and head straight to the fish and chip shops. The fish and chips would be wrapped in newspaper and consumed before reaching home, as everyone knows they always tasted better in newspaper.

HIGH STREET (WHITEHEADS)

On turning the corner into the High Street was one of the big Grocery Shops and Bakeries; Whiteheads. It wasn't until later years I had the opportunity to visit the bakery. On walking into this 'hot house' was Mr Loll (Laurence) Clarke. A very friendly man who showed me how he made bread and how it turned out after being in the ovens.

From one end of the High Street to the other the two main shops belonged to the Bunting Family, they were commonly known as Top Buntings and Bottom Buntings. When I worked as a junior at Top Buntings, every morning around 10 o'clock I was sent down to Bottom Buntings for bread which was ordered by customers at the Top Buntings. Carrying two heavy old fashioned bread baskets on each arm I would come back loaded with bread. The weather didn't come into it, sun, rain, hail, snow; the bread had to be fetched ready to be added to the orders going out into the country by the grocery man, Jack Keyte, every day. There was no other smell like fresh bread coming out of the oven.

At the time I used to go to the Baptist Church in Henley Street. When it was Harvest Festival, Mr Clark would make a wheat sheaf and give it to me to place on the altar as my contribution for the service. How we all miss his home made bread and cakes. His goods travelled all around the district. Mr Clark worked for the famous Charles Bunting (bottom shop). Mrs Bunting, his wife, was affectionately called 'Mother' by Charles. Often he would be heard shouting 'MOTHER!' and Mrs Charles, as townspeople knew her, would always reply with a lovely red glow on her face and seemed as happy as anyone could be. The staff were very loyal: Jean Steed, Jean Cusack and Ken Palmer were always there to greet you. The shop was constantly a hub of activity, one of the most popular in the town.

THE SMALLER SHOPS

What do we have next? Buggin's flower, fruit and veg shop. Again the flower shop was very small, but packed with glorious flowers and plants. It was a joy to have such personal attention by any of the family or Sylvia Palmer who also worked there and knew exactly what customers wanted. The secrets they must have kept concerning weddings and funerals!

We have no cobblers in Alcester now but Sammy Preece was one of two that were in the town, Don Holmes being the other. The strong smell of leather greeted you as you walked in the door to the compact counter. Sam would appear, a dark wavy haired gent wearing his brown overall.

Sammy had a window display of mainly Dinky toys which were most popular at the end of the week, as a reward for children from their parents if they had been good. Rows of shoes to be mended were always on show by the great machine. No-one left the shop without listening to a 'story' that Sam would tell, always making the locals leave laughing and in good spirits.

One thing that has not changed is next door to Sammy's shop. This was the windows of Collette Café', still the same today, but now the successful Orange Mabel Tearooms. Mrs Brice and her daughter Mary ran the café for many years. Cyclists and passers by regularly called in, it was a treat to sit in the window and watch the world go by. Mary would come and ask you in a very motherly voice 'what would we like?' Strawberry milkshake it had to be. To see the coffee being made, the teas being poured and the whisking of our milkshake being made just for us. Pure heaven on a hot day. A very busy establishment.

MANCHESTER HOUSE

Apart from the local Co-op in Evesham Street, the only other large clothes shop was Manchester House. The well known character there was Mrs Doll Croft, she would wait to serve you with great interest as to why and who you were buying for. After finding out she would say, eyes wide open, 'Oh I see!' With an eager look waiting to hear any more news. She would then continue to find just the right thing at the right price. I guess the store room was up the winding, highly polished stairs stood in the middle of the shop, but most garments were kept in drawers either behind the counter or underneath. 'Crofty', as she was affectionately called, could be seen working in many types of establishments over the years.

ADCOCK'S CHEMIST

Mr Jim Adcock! (Adcock's Chemist). Well now what can we say about this great man? He celebrated 100 years of family business in 1972. Here he stood behind the pharmacy counter making prescriptions up, a tall slender man, wearing half glasses with pure white hair. His staff, all ladies, were Miss Dianna Mainwaring, Mrs Margaret Handy, Sandra King and Joyce Coles. Each learnt the art of knowing how to help with customers ailments.

No matter how nasty your cough was, Mr Adcock would cure it with his own magic potion. Within days you would feel better. No need to go to the Doctor, you would see a babies weighing scale in there should anyone wish to have their baby weighed.

The shop was surrounded with massive green and blue jars on the top shelves, depicting the old fashioned chemist. A wooden slatted shelf stretched across the counter for the shopper to rest their bags. On leaving the shop after his day's work he would be seen with his long coat and trilby hat walking home to Acorn House, Evesham Street. Mr Adcock, along with many others of that era, was made High Bailiff of Alcester Court Leet whilst working in the shop. A quiet pleasant gent and always most polite, Mr Adcock was in many organisations in the town for many years and was often seen supporting them for years after. One of the great men to be respected and remembered.

PETE BAYLISS FRUIT AND VEG

A small but very useful shop, very compact with fresh fruit and veg. Every morning the display of goods were carried out, always of high quality. A notice was displayed on the tomatoes saying 'PLEASE DON'T SQUEEZE ME UNTIL I'M YOURS'! If Pete Bayliss saw anyone squeezing the tomatoes he would discreetly add that particular tomato when weighing them into the bag.

Like many shops at the time, the toilet was down the bottom of the garden. No chain to pull so a bucket of water had to be carried there each time you needed the loo! It was fun working there as a young girl. Each time any young single gentleman came in to buy, Pete would have a bet on how long the conversation would last between me and whoever the gentleman was before we actually went out for the evening. Rightly or wrongly he encouraged me many times to see if anything came of it!

THE LOCAL PHOTOGRAPHER

Next door was the famous Wilf Smith. Mr Smith was the local photographer, as well as playing the violin and clarinet in Alcester Light Orchestra at the local Town Hall. The only real entertainment to look forward to in the 50s was the Saturday night dance at the Town Hall. A large rounded man, balding on the top, who always wore round glasses, a short tweed waistcoat and his famous watch hanging from his pocket. The

Local photographer Wilf Smith.

main shop door was painted brown, during opening hours he would open the top of the door to leave the bottom half closed and lean across it watching the world go by and chat with anyone passing by.

It was quite a dark shop inside with a flagstone floor. On entering a small bell would ring and if he wasn't leaning on the door he would come from out of the back of the shop wearing his flat cap, round glasses and carrying his walking stick.

He also made homemade wine as a hobby. On one occasion he asked me to try some damson wine which I thought was a nice gesture. It nearly blew my head off but being polite I said how nice it was. The next day he brought me some more, but I hadn't the heart to say it was too strong so I tipped it down the nearest drain when he wasn't looking!

GEORGE MASON

George Mason's, or the Star as it was sometimes called, was a grocery shop that dominated the centre of the High Street. The green and yellow sign stood high for all to see. The Hemming sisters all worked there: June, Dolly, Marj and Gertie. Looking through the large window one or other could be seen slicing the bacon or cutting the cheeses. It was a long shop with most of the groceries on shelves behind the counter.

Orders were delivered regularly. There was always a chair in the main shop. One time a poor lady 'Fag End Annie' as she was known, was taken ill and escorted to sit on the chair. She was often seen in a long black gown looking in the gutters every morning for cigarette ends. I believe she was taken to hospital and never heard of again.

YOU CAN GET IT AT BUNTINGS

The rich and the poor were always welcomed and looked after. Groceries were packed by staff and carried out to cars. 'Crofty' (the lady mentioned previously) as she was known, seemed to fill in helping out at most shops, adapting to wherever she was needed. In the 60s, at Christmas she was to be seen behind a table of Whiteways wines offering free samples of Cherry, Peach and Apricot wine for the customers in Buntings Grocer and Delicatessen shop. This was her job to ask customers if they would like to sample one of the flavours in the hope they would buy a bottle. The Peach wine was hidden under the table, as that was the favourite. When the staff passed by she would give them a sample during the Christmas rush of customers' orders. It was quickly knocked back before the boss, John Bunting or his family, saw us.

Buntings was a high class shop selling everything you could think of to do with food, their motto was 'You can get it at Buntings'.

It was such a joy to be working there, especially at Christmas. Shelves were decorated at night after the day's work. The boss would always leave us light refreshment of gin and tonic to keep us going. The shop had that Christmas spirit about it. Each room had something different to tempt the customer. There was always Santa's Grotto, tucked away in one of the smaller rooms, with Father Christmas, of course, giving away little delights out of his big red sack for the children.

The shop was like a maze, there was always somewhere to hide, you could go through one of the doors, down the damp cellar which curved round, and come out the other end of the shop if you didn't want to be found, especially with the opposite gender! We would hear the boss's whistle or even hear him shout 'Has anyone seen Maggie?' That was when the cellar was most useful. In one door, down the cement steps, run through the racks of wine up the other end to the steps leading to the middle of the shop… then announce 'Here I am did you want me?'

Every evening at 5 o'clock, a gentleman who was known as 'Gaffer' or Mr Shervington would arrive with his leather gaiters on. He was a very quiet but happy man with rosy cheeks and a smile that widened if we told him we were making a cup of tea. His job was to burn all the empty boxes at the bottom of Buntings garden each evening. On one occasion one of the part time boys came into work slightly worse for wear. It was obvious he couldn't work as he tried so hard to push trolleys round and he was sent home. As the day wore on, some staff were leaving the shop and found the same boy fast asleep recovering from his night out very close to the bonfire that was due to be lit! Needless to say he lived to see another day.

The errand boy would arrive after school, load his bike up and off he would go delivering orders in all weathers. The old fashioned bicycle with the large tilted basket in front was used as soon as the schools finished for the day. I well remember Brian Jones coming from school to deliver goods locally come rain or shine.

It was a fascinating building with lots of nooks and crannies, a wonderful cellar and large outside warehouses, one of which was where the toilet rolls were kept, on top of tall iron steps leading to an old building. The only way to get them to the room was for one to throw and another to catch. The large warehouse where almost everything in the grocery line was kept had many tales to tell! Again the giant cereal boxes were thrown up the old wooden stairs into a loft. When needed a large hatch was opened and they were thrown back down again to fill the fixtures in the shop. Catapults could be found left on the shelf in the main warehouse, after an elderly member of staff had sat and tried to get the squirrels in the garden. In the stone flagged kitchen rabbits were hanging from the ceiling and an old fashioned washer stood in the corner, ready for the housekeeper (Mrs Flanny Keyte) to use. Many times we would see a misty face through the hot steam coming from the mangle.

It was such an experience to enter a world I had never known existed. On leaving work the staff were offered a glass of sherry from out of the old fashioned sherry barrels. It was an establishment where staff were treated as family and well looked after.

'A shop for all seasons' as the notice said on top of the shop door, behind the golden sugar loaf, hanging with pride.

Old fashioned mangle.

ALCESTER CINEMA

Dominating the High Street was the local Cinema. Lol Rouse and Charlie Lawman pioneered the running of the films and Marian Trout was the usherette who soon put you in your place if any trouble was caused. Seeing the shining light from Marian's torch, you knew someone was going to get a warning or even thrown out.

When the top films were on, it was frustrating to stand outside and not be able to go in because you were either too young or couldn't afford it. The queue to get in and see a newly released film would stretch down the High Street. When the doors opened there was lots of pushing and shoving to get a good seat, especially for the courting couples who always wanted upstairs in the back row.

Often children would go round knocking on doors asking for empty lemonade or beer bottles to return to the local pubs and then get money back, so they could afford to go to the Cinema or 'Flicks' as it was known. Obviously children could not get in unless accompanied by an adult, so we were almost begging the older people to let us go with them. It didn't work very well!

Wendy Weatherhead (née Grummett) recalls that they showed three different programmes a week; Monday for three nights, Thursday for three nights, Sunday one night and a children's film on Saturday morning for 6 pence. It was 1 shilling and 3 pence to go on the balcony, she had 5 shillings a week pocket money and spent it all on the films. Lol Rouse and Lou Devey were the projectionists. Folk who came into town to go to the pictures on their bikes stored them at Mrs Horton's alley next to 32 high street for 1 shilling. Before there were regular films shown the cinema had been a concert hall.

BOWENS

On the same side of the High Street was Mr Bowen's quaint little shop, selling everything the housewife needed from carpets, curtains, dusters and tea towels to bed linen. The shop is still very much the same today as it was then, with Richard Bowen serving behind the counter. There was a showroom in the middle of the High Street with furniture in which that could be purchased from Bowens shop.

Between Bowens shop and the Cinema were rows of cottages with lovely bay windows. Nothing was private as you passed by seeing the residents sat in their living rooms. Very few had net curtains up to deter anyone from looking in. Vandals were not heard of then!

The cottages were a handy place to live in the centre of the High Street.

ELECTRICAL SHOPS

There were three local Electrical shops almost opposite each other, one was run by Mr Curtis next to the Bear Inn. A variety of electrical goods would be strewn around the small shop all waiting to be repaired. The other shop was Wrights which also sold local records, Mr and Mrs Wright were the proprietors with a young man named Tony as their assistant. All the latest 'hits' of the day were advertised in the window, anything from the Everley Brothers and Helen Shapiro to Cliff Richard. When Christmas came round their record players were highly sought after as gifts.

Burdens was the well-known family-run shop, although you could get almost anything there to fix DIY jobs. David Burden was also often seen attending shops that needed help with lighting.

WAITING AT THE BUS STOP

We must not forget the two Miss Hemmings whose cottage stood right by the bus stop. In the window were small children's toys which they had made. Often children tired of waiting for the bus would stand and look into the window wishing and wondering! Nurse Buckley also lived there and was often seen riding her large brown horse through the town with matching long brown coat, on her rounds as a midwife. She was also often seen doing her shopping with a cigarette in her mouth as she walked down the High Street.

LOCAL BUTCHERS

If you walked down the High Street early in the morning you would find shop keepers sweeping the front pavement, some with buckets of hot soapy water to make doubly sure the entrance to their shops was welcoming. The butchers carefully strewing sawdust on the highly cleaned mosaic floor tiles. Stan Snow and Reg Grummett (both with their own butchers shop) always had a cheery smile as you looked in their doorways on passing. Stan with his mother standing in the background, a white-haired lady with shiny cheeks, ready to oblige. Reg could often be heard to say 'now let's see what we have for you'. Either he, or Ted Taylor or Keith Grummett (Reggie's son), would know what the customer required. Shops with wooden floors were carefully being sprinkled with water before sweeping the dust off and bringing the meat out.

THE CENTRE OF THE HIGH STREET

Early morning, Hairdressers would be cleaning their windows so passersby could see the beauty of having their hair treated in the shop. In the centre of the High Street was a ladies hairdresser owned by Mrs Lincoln. Her hair was grey and always tied in a bun at the back. She wore bright red lipstick and gold dangling ear rings. As children we dreaded having our hair cut as she seemed to love those clippers that would bite the back of your neck as she glided them up and down. Further up was The Seed Shop, run by dear Mrs Hopkins and her husband, Ron. Every wild seed imaginable was on display. Like so many of the shops, each had its different aroma as you walked in the door.

In the centre of the town one of the biggest shops was *The Chronicle* Office (now Barclays Bank). A large building that sold every newspaper and magazine possible. Everyone looked forward to Friday morning and the delivery of the local paper. Mrs Gallimore Senior, with her silvery white hair placed the newspapers out methodically on the long counter, *The Alcester Chronicle* being the most popular. One of the busiest shops in the High Street, Mr Portman (senior) also worked there, even when he retired.

The Alcester Chronicle newspaper was jam packed with local news. This was all down to a gentleman called Aubrey Gwinnett. He would often be seen walking around the town looking and asking for news, even visiting organisations in the evening to report back to the newspaper. He would call into the local butcher, Reg Grummett, for news on the Council and what went on with the local football team. At the time *The Alcester Chronicle* was always full of Alcester news, all thanks to Aubrey Gwinnett.

Opposite *The Chronicle* Office was Alcester Builders. Many years ago Albert James made the coffins out of wood shavings, sawdust and glue pots on a stove. In later years he did suffer with his breathing. Is it any wonder!

MORE SHOPS

Adkins Men's Wear and Mrs Butler's shop stood next to each other. Two delightful looking shops, with smartly dressed mannequins in the window. Again both were family run businesses.

Next, was another small grocer shop called 'Moggs'. Mrs Peachey was often seen slicing bacon in the front window first thing in the morning. A few years afterwards it turned into a shoe shop, the owner was Miss Allan, followed by the local Norman Cole, and to date the Humphries family, who are still there today. Many Alcestrians will remember the very same shop as children.

Next door a window of sparkling jewellery was displayed by the Wilkes family whose jewellery shop was always a joy to look into. The only times I was taken in there was by an old aunt who treated me occasionally. I believe this was due to my parents allowing her to live with them after

Aubrey Gwinnett as a Court Leet Member.

'something went wrong' with her family for what seemed an age! My mother was promised the earth for taking her in, but we never saw or heard of her again when she left.

Next door was Colletts, more of a confectionery shop at the time, although they did sell newspapers and magazines.

Mrs Drew, such a lovely, well-dressed lady owned a tiny Ladies Wear shop (now a Chinese take-away). Meticulously clean inside, the shop always had something to sell as gifts or dress wear. As an easy, acceptable present Mrs Drew would have beautifully displayed handkerchiefs in boxes. Many excuses were used to go and buy something from her shop during the girls working hours. Such a stylish and pleasant lady.

Mr Stanley was a well-known character in the High Street who owned an Ironmonger's shop. He would be seen putting his bright, shiny dustbins out for sale in a meticulous row. The shop always smelt of paraffin which he kept in the back of the shop. On entering the premises, the radio would be on and you would smell the smoke from his tobacco getting nearer and wonder how on earth the establishment never caught fire. On more than one occasion customers would go in and ask for something and his answer was 'I've just this minute run out, it will be in next week'. The times we heard that phrase. He was a very polite gentleman even if you weren't a regular customer. His dustbins were regularly displayed out on the frontage.

Alcester High Street was famous for the family establishments, Buntings, Burdens, Buggins and Bowens. Known as 'All the Bs'. All these businesses continued to work for many more years in the town.

CHURCH STREET AND HENLEY STREET

On the corner of Church Street, at the top of Malt Mill Lane, the other cobbler was Don Holmes. He was always thorough in his work. Next door was a beautiful gift shop which he also owned. The sort that sold high quality gifts for that special person. The glass ornaments would glisten as you looked around to purchase a gift and Don would always try and advise on the right gift to buy.

In the 50s many shops sold all sorts of things for convenience. One such shop was owned by Phil and Arthur Wilkes in Henley Street. This surely must have been a great favourite for all sorts of reasons! As you walked in you could see the door where they actually lived during the day. Out would come Phyliss asking 'what would you like today my duck?' She would wait patiently while we decided what we, as children, could buy. We thought nothing of running from Ten Acres, down Gunnings Road to fetch soap powder or paraffin from this lovely shop for our mothers. Anything and everything could be found in this Aladdin's Cave. Arthur Wilkes would be seen on Saturday mornings driving round in an old fashioned green van, parking in most streets. If you needed anything household, Mr Wilkes was the man who had it. Out of the driver's seat he would get, dressed in his khaki overall and release the shutters either side of the van, where anything from soap to candles could be purchased. In those days you never knew when there would be a power cut so candles and paraffin were a must to keep in the house.

Rumour has it that on certain nights Arthur would go to church choir practise and invite Eric Payne and friends who were also in the choir, to the back of the shop for a tot of whisky. One can only imagine what stories they must have shared!

MRS KENDALL'S CAKES

Always on a Friday during the school holidays I never minded going shopping as my mother and I always called in at the corner shop (now a hairdressers) and I was treated to a iced bun. A most tempting shop, full of the nicest cakes you ever did see, but an iced bun was what I got. Although I had six brothers I don't recall them ever having one, maybe I was the favoured one! Mrs Kendall was a smart, dark-haired lady who often wore a cross over pinafore. Some time after, Mr and Mrs Goss took over and also opened up a Café at the back entrance in Meeting Lane. The juke box was always playing and many teenagers were seen jiving to the latest songs.

THINGS TO DO

On a warm day people were often seen walking from the Conway Estate to the top of Birmingham Road into the Grammar School field and onto the old railway line. Walking full circle of the town, stopping on the way to walk through 'Ghost Wood' or even paddle in the river, this was a favourite place for many who lived in the town. In the summer months families took picnics there whilst children paddled in the polluted water under the great iron bridge!

Games were played; boys on rusty bikes would be seen riding over the hilly parts. This was a wonderful place to be with friends. Young couples could be seen embracing under the bridges.

Carrying on walking along the extensive railway track to nearby Great Alne we would pass the famous Jimmy Adams Nursery, and could always

The old iron bridge.

either see or hear him bellowing over the fields to his workers, his was a voice everyone knew. Jim never refused anyone a job on his land, especially the young in the school holidays. His vast greenhouses overflowing with plants were a credit to him. The radiance of the chrysanthemum blooms, yellow, gold, white and burgundy all ready for autumn. On Saturday mornings a stall would be set out to sell either tiny tomatoes or reject tomatoes with all the other salad ingredients. A local man producing local food.

Continuing along the track, half way to the other end was a bridge which was called the Sandbanks, mainly for the colour of the soil. We would often stop under the bridge for a rest in the peace and quiet of a summer's day. That was until the farmer, Mr Kinnersley, would guide his cows across the bridge to another field. The sound of thunder from the cows hooves gave us such a shock, we would slide down the red sandbanks, laughing our heads off, until I suddenly realised I had my best frilly knickers on that were bought for my birthday from my mother! These beautiful frilly knickers were covered in red sand. Too scared to go home and show the underwear, I took them off and put them in one of the bins on the way home. The following night explaining to my mother, after I had a bath, that I couldn't find my new knickers anywhere to put on and that SHE must have lost them! How bad is that?

The river flowed through to the other end of town to Oversley where the river backed onto Arrow, another place to go where many of the older boys were to be found. A long thick rope hung from one of the great oak trees and the boys would climb the tree, swinging on the rope and jumping into the water, known as the Basin. I guess because of the shape of it. On one occasion, my friend decided to paddle in the water and was stuck by a whirl pool. Her one leg went down into the pool, leaving her screaming for help! Some gallant gentleman jumped in and pulled her out minus a black shoe.

As very young children the age old game of cowboys and indians was played, especially by the small wood which backed onto our houses. Dens were made in the local woods out of branches and greenery. Blankets, bottles of fruit drinks and biscuits which had been sneaked out of the house all went into our Den. Any friends who wanted to join us had to guess a password first. How cruel was that? They could stand there for quite a while until they guessed the right password.

We had to wait for the older boys, be nice to them and ask them to make bows and arrows for us from branches off the trees, so that we could charge through the wood and outlying areas looking for the 'cowboys'.

It wasn't uncommon to sit on the kerb of the main road with a note book and pen and write down all the registration numbers of cars as they passed. These must have been very boring days when few children were about to play with as it was holiday time.

One particular day my friend and I wondered what it was like to smoke a cigarette. We thought if we bought a box of drinking straws and tightly pushed grass inside we would know! We crept into her parents' shed, locked the door, lit the drinking straw, nothing happened. We tried again and oh dear Lord, smoke everywhere! We couldn't find the lock to undo the door so were quietly choking in case anyone heard us. We never tried it again!

There were plenty of long walks that would take us anywhere with no fear of anything happening to us. If you didn't own a bike you would borrow a neighbour's and ride for hours round the district.

Games played in the road were popular in the evening until gradually, on odd nights, some of us would slope off with 'other' friends. I guess this was the start of growing up!

Roads were used for all sorts of games in the 50s and 60s. Many times chalk was used to write on the road and play hopscotch. There was always an empty tin to be found to play Tin Can Alley. Ball games were played, not always the best thing if the ball went over into someone's garden. Out would come the occasional neighbour threatening if it happened again we wouldn't have the ball back. Of course it did happen again so someone was nominated to crawl through the hedge to retrieve the ball from the garden. One little old lady would come out with glasses of lemonade for us children on hot nights.

For some time there was a craze of playing marbles. How envious we were of those that had the big Dollers! We tried so hard to buy them off the big boys but they wouldn't have it!

The summer days were always hot so many were seen out walking by the rivers. It wasn't unusual to see young girls just sitting on the grass and making daisy chains, this was a 'project' until the chain broke and then we moved on. Simple things to pass the time away in the sunny weather.

During the six week holidays I used to enjoy listening to the Everly Brothers songs with my friend Anne, who lived at the top of Ten Acres. Anne's mother would go to work and we would spend hours listening to the records on her record player, drinking coffee with not a care in the world. We actually believed they were singing to us! It was at the time when all the local boys were Teddy boys, dressed in their black jackets adorned with glitter, tight jeans and winkle-picker shoes.

It was in the early 60s new entertainment was found in Meeting Lane. The tenants had a bread shop in Henley Street but used the large back room for a café with a juke box. Many times I tried to get in there and actually stay but my brother Phillip wasn't having any of it (brother and sister attitude at the time) yet it was wonderful to watch those older than me rocking and rolling.

The Hemming brothers from Ten Acres were continuously playing cricket, but they were lucky enough to have a large area of grass between them and the road. Mr Hemming senior would lean against the gate and hold a friendly conversation.

In the same road Mr Sreeves lived on the corner. He was always in his garden which had a lovely display of flowers. Every night when I went out he would wait for me, comment on my dress and inquire where and who I was going to see, then tell me to be careful who I brought home!

THE CHIMNEY SWEEP AND COALMAN

Who could forget the local Chimney Sweep, Joe Archer? I was fascinated to watch him get his utensils together, placing sheets all round the fireplace. He would chat away to me asking if I liked school and what was I going to do when I grew up? The answer was always the same! Ironically I said 'work in a shop', where to date, I work now! Even though we only saw him annually he would always say 'Hello' when he saw you out.

There was much intrigue in watching your parents 'draw' the fire with a sheet of newspaper to get the fire going and then complain there was too much 'slack'.

It's hard to believe that you would have to light the fire when you had woken up to frost sticking to the windows and you couldn't see outside for the many patterns the ice had formed. The coalman, Paddy Sherlock, was a regular visitor. As he passed the kitchen window he would shout 'How many this week Mrs?'

Another hard working gentleman who regularly called was the man who collected the 'pig swill' to feed his pigs on Sunday mornings. He must have known every house in town.

Joe Archer the Chimney Sweep.

CHARACTERS

At precisely 8.50am in the morning the two Gittus brothers would be seen walking down the Birmingham Road together to work at the local Co-op Offices in Evesham Street. They were smartly dressed in their trench coats and always 'tipping' their hats to say 'Good Morning', even though they didn't know me!

Shops in those days seemed to keep their staff for years. Mrs Betts, who worked at the chemist could be seen smartly setting out in her brogue lace up shoes with a Cuban heel, dead on 8.50am in the morning from the prefab where she lived.

'Little Tommy Jones' the window cleaner, was everybody's friend. His shrill 'Hallo!' to all the locals could be heard even if he was cleaning windows and he couldn't see who was behind him. Tom carried his own small ladder on his shoulders, I think he only did lower windows. For many years he lived with his sister and an older lady, who wore a long black skirt, and could be seen every morning beating the dust out of the carpet against their front wall in Ten Acres. On many nights I would come home late and see Tommy's house all lit up with Christmas lights even in the middle of summer.

'Old Tom' was another character, a tall slim gentleman often with an empty crate under his arm and wearing a long beige coat, he would parade up and down the High Street after leaving the little cottage he lived in with his mother in Henley Street. He would make his way up the Stratford Road to 'work' in the fields. No one ever seemed to know what this work was.

In later years I had the pleasure of helping a friend out who moved into the very same cottage. I chose to dig the garden, only to find loads of medicine bottles still with the mixture in and dentures that had obviously never been used but thrown out or hidden in the garden by Tom or his mother.

Another character was Geoff Spires, he would welcome anyone in to see his fine medals and photos of him as a young man hanging on the wall. On inquiring how he was, his answer was always the same, 'Happy as a Dead Bird!'

Of course, every town has a 'Molly and Queenie'. Two very well-known characters who were often seen at Civic dinners, parties and joining in with any street celebration. Molly and Queenie were the two reliable people to call upon to do the washing up. Not just for a few people but for anyone who asked. That was, of course, if they were not already booked beforehand. All they asked for was a 'Thank you' and if they could possibly take some food home with them. Cups, saucers, plates, dishes and glasses were left scrupulously clean.

Usually seen in the same vicinity was Doris Wilkes in her smart black and white uniform, serving the food. Doris was married to Harry. Another couple who joined in most of the Towns activities. Harry loved dancing, especially Barn Dancing. He would often ask me to dance with him but sadly, his feet didn't go with mine and we would end up laughing more than dancing! To this day I still have marks on my legs where his feet didn't quite touch the floor!

Often as children we were sent to a local seamstress for clothes alterations for the family. A little French lady, Mrs Young was her name, greeted us at the door in Priory Road. No one could understand a word she said so instructions had to be written down on paper. We dreaded the opening of her front door as the aroma was something else! A lot of nodding 'yes' went on as we couldn't understand her, but the clothing always came back perfect, she did a wonderful job.

There seemed to be quite a few older people who loved a good night out at the pub but unfortunately found it hard to walk home. One evening I was walking home and could hear a kind of grumbling and chuntering going on. There, coming over the local bridge were a couple finding their way back home. The gentleman had no shoes or socks on and was walking sideways with splayed feet, while his wife was walking behind and shouting, 'TURN LEFT, TURN LEFT YOU FOOL!' The next day the very same gent was seen riding his bike into town again at an angle but was never run over!

Bleachfield Street, apparently, was the poorest but the best street in town. The men were often seen going to the pub at night and coming home full of beer, shouting and swearing at each other. Come the next morning they were all the best of friends. Children listening in fear in their bedrooms would wait to hear 'Jack the Snob' (that was his nickname) returning home. Apparently this gentleman only had one leg so everyone knew it was him by the single tap of his foot. Sunday mornings were a favourite for one gentleman who would walk along the town picking up loose change that the drunks had dropped out of their pockets the previous night. I believe the popular drink in those days was mainly cider.

The Bleachfield Street celebrations were the best in town, remembering this was a poor area, they always made the most effort for any celebration with strings of bunting stretching from window to window.

LOCAL PUBS

The local pubs always seemed to be full especially at weekends. Groups could be seen playing cards, darts or dominoes through the windows of the The Turk's Head, The Lord Nelson or The Hollybush. Other pubs which had a piano would be heaving with people singing to the local pianist. When he tired of playing, another pint of beer was placed on the piano and off he would go again, with a new lease of life.

Len Wilkes would be at the Globe Hotel and he would get his wife, Emily, to come down and they would entertain the punters. Always a great treat.

The Bell Inn did a mean Welsh rarebit at the weekends, the best you ever tasted. The Royal Oak was run by Kath Jobson a lovely lady who managed the pub really well for many years. Every morning, she could be seen sweeping the pavement at 9 o'clock on the dot.

George Boyce was another well-known character who was to be seen in the pubs every night. His last destination was the Lord Nelson in Priory Road. He was only a small man but could pack away many a pint of beer. He would walk in and say he had just been to Spernall Duck Races where Khaki Campbell came first, I really believed him! On leaving the pub he would say 'Watch where they settle'! Who or what he meant I never knew.

As a young girl, one Sunday morning, I was early coming out of Sunday School and decided to walk home through the town and not go straight home. I passed the Bear Hotel where there were two open doors facing the main road in the High Street and you

George Boyce.

could see men sat on stools at the bar. I suddenly caught sight of my father and shouted 'Dad, can I come in?' He nearly fell off the stool! His hand went into his pocket and out came a 2 shilling piece. He said to keep it secret and not to tell my mother that I had seen him that morning when I got home! Always on Sundays lunchtime was at 1 o'clock, listening to Billy Cotton's Band Show on the wireless. More often than not we had a Sunday roast and some sort of home made pudding. My father would rarely finish his dinner because of being in The Bear beforehand! I kept that secret but my mother knew all the time why he couldn't finish his meal. Sometimes he would bring home a box of Cadbury's Flat Twenties as a peace offering to Mum.

The Globe Pub was stuck in the middle of the division of the Evesham Road and Birmingham Road and had a lovely area outside to sit out in during the summer evenings. Len Chambers used to play his accordion and sing songs in the Globe Hotel on a Saturday night, "With me gloves in me hand, and me hat on one side"! Len was also a very public figure in the church; if any job wanted doing Len was your man.

My mother was in hospital for a good six weeks during the 50s so I was taken in to live with a neighbour. My mother said there was no way I could stop at home with seven men in the house (my father and six older brothers) while she was away recuperating! On Saturdays the Odell family took me and their daughter Janet to the Globe Hotel. It was a real treat to go to the Public house, sit outside and eat crisps with a bottle of Vimto. Other times we would go to the Cross Keys and although it had a smaller court yard it was just as nice watching the regulars go in and the banter that went on. It was something my mother would never allow, to be seen in or outside a public house. How times changed in later years!

The Red Horse was run by the unique couple Gertie and Tom Houghton. I say unique because there was never a married couple like them. Pure gems. It was a very popular pub, at the weekend they would have entertainment nights. I guess even then you could call them Karaoke nights! I remember, yes, sadly standing on a table with a gentleman singing Sonny and Cher's song 'I got you Babe'!

On another occasion I was going out with a gentleman and had instructions to go to the Red Horse and meet him that evening. I was too eager so arrived far too early. While I was waiting and talking to Tom, a coach load of people appeared. Tom said 'Quick, go and find Gertie in the living quarters and tell her I need help'. I went looking in every room. No Gertie! I rushed back into the pub, told Tom who promptly said 'well you will have to help me, get behind the bar'! I had never pulled a pint in my life! However, within minutes in walked Gertie through the front door wearing a beautiful sun hat and floral dress. Tom said, 'we have been looking for you, where have you been?' Gertie, God Bless her said 'Oh I caught the 8 o'clock coach to Weston Super Mare this morning!' She had been gone all day and he hadn't missed her! On visiting her for afternoon tea, she would give you cake that was three weeks out of date, but you ate it so as not to offend!

CHURCHES

From the age of five, I was sent to the Baptist Chapel where Mr Cox was the Minister. I don't remember much, except going there morning, afternoon and night! Each year they held the Annual Anniversary and we had to practise with Mr Lol Clarke to sing solos for this special Sunday. Would you believe we were allowed to wear a 'special' dress for that day?

Just before Easter a group of us children would walk up Cold Comfort Lane with a picnic to find primroses in the wood to decorate the church. We would find a long stick, pick bunches of primroses and tie them with wool to the long stick. Then we would sit in the wood and have our picnic before walking back home to the Baptist Church. The next day we would fill the church with primroses ready for the Easter Sunday Services.

I stayed until my teens as I desperately wanted the main prize of the Bible which I considered I had earned over the years, never missing a Sunday. I continued going to the Baptist Chapel then decided to move over to St Nicholas Church across the road. When I told my mother she said, 'you needn't think you are being confirmed until you have been there at least 12 months'. I ventured over there to try it out, I sat in the congregation at first but then decided to join the choir.

It was mainly Evensong in the 50s and 60s. Choir practise was held every Tuesday Evening at 7.30 prompt. Talking in-between practising was not allowed. Mr Steed would turn round from his piano seat, look down his glasses and say 'Who is that talking?' You knew choir practise was for singing, nothing else.

When sitting in the choir stalls for services. There was always a strong smell of mints. Jim Simonds (Rev now) would often poke us in the back to share what we had stashed away in the choir pews.

One evening my dear friend Esme was wearing contact lenses. As we were about to sit down after singing a hymn, she whispered, 'be careful where you put your feet, my contact lens has fallen out of my eye'! There we were trying to be discreet in looking on the floor for this contact lens when the Rev Emrys Jones announced, 'We will now sing the hymn Thy Hand O God has guided'. We had to stand up and sing it… but whether the hymn gave us inspiration or not, we suddenly saw what looked like a tear drop glistening on the floor. It was the contact lens!

Sometimes, as young girls often do, you find something to amuse you, and find it very hard to stop laughing. One such time was when the choir were proceeding around the church before the service started and the person carrying the cross forgot to look out for the chandelier. There was such a clank, the chandelier was swinging backwards and forwards, it looked like something out of a comedy film. It just tickled us, we just couldn't stop laughing, and tears were rolling down our faces. By the time we had reached the choir stalls, where the congregation could see us, I had to turn my head and face the altar as I knew the Rev Emrys Jones who sat next to me would wonder what on earth was the matter with me. As it was, he told me afterwards that he could see what I was doing, but contained myself very professionally!

It was always the highlight to see all Rev Emrys Jones' family attending church, maybe because their son Michael was unattached! What a let down when the choir held a buffet and dance one year! I was all geared up wishing

so badly to see a certain person. He never turned up but an apology was
sent by his father.

I was at an age when men became very interesting. Choir girls realised
it wasn't all boring being in the church choir. Many parties were held after
church services in the Butler boy's garden in Kings Coughton. Lights were
lit in all the trees in their orchard and food was plentiful. They were always

*St Nicholas Choir. Back Row: Jim Symonds, Vic Butler, Eric Payne, Mick Mills,
Pete Harman and Pete Butler. Second Row from the back: Peter Short,
Roger???? Arthur Wilkes. Third Row from the Back: Marie Symonds, Chris
Haines, Esme Evans, Beryl Haines (in front of Chris Haines), Janice Baldwin,
Jennifer Smith, moving round to the centre is Jenny Payne, Maggie Pick,
Charlotte Collins, Valerie Haines, Hilda Daffern, Jean Steed, Rita Butler.
Youngsters in the front: Simon Wateley, Chris Saunders, Martin Payne, Chris
Steed, David Wall, Steven Febrey, Nick Steed, Robert Stanton, Susan Easton,
Chris Febrey, Peter Blundell, Irene Payne. Front Row: Bill Roberts, Norman
Steed, Rev Emrys Jones, Baden Wheeler.*

nights to remember. We did have a young man join the choir whose name was Henry. Now I think I was set up as one thing led to another and after becoming very friendly with Henry from the choir he appeared in the shop where I worked. He drew up about 5.30pm in a bright yellow sports car, walked into the shop and said to my boss 'Could I take Margaret home please?' My boss, usually quite strict with closing at 6 o'clock, saw the car and this refined gentleman and said 'I see no reason why she can't leave work early'. I was shocked!

Off we went in the little yellow car, going straight past the road in which I lived and parked up in a hidden lay by! First we chatted and then another car appeared, I made the excuse it was a local policeman who was a neighbour. Needless to say we drove off and Henry dropped me off at my house with me promising to see him again. Thankfully he left the district the following weekend! Maybe I scared him off!

Christmas was always a lovely time in the church choir. Apart from the many carol services, we would go out carol singing to certain people's houses. Two of which I remember were Angel House where Caroline and Mike Newey would produce hot mulled wine after, and onto The Field House in Cold Comfort Lane where Mr and Mrs Norman lived. Again more mulled wine. The last visit was to the Rev Anne and Arthur Stally's home. A massive, beautifully lit Christmas tree was in the lounge with hot drinks and mince pies waiting for us.

It became apparent that we could actually get more money if we went round the pubs too. Mr Steed wasn't that keen but after I said I would go round with the tin, he agreed. What fantastic takings! It became an annual event after that.

Midnight Mass was always a special occasion. One year my friend Esme and I decided to go to the Bear Hotel in the High Street and have a quiet drink beforehand. The open wood fire was glowing all around the room. We ordered our drinks and time rolled on until we realised we should be moving on to church for the late service. To our surprise, whilst we had been sat in The Bear pub, snow had fallen very deeply! Now we all know sitting in a very warm room, drinking alcohol and going out into the bitter cold is not a good thing before going to church! We decided to walk around the town for a while to clear our heads. At this point I should mention that Rev Stally had decided to take his enormous white dog for a walk before the service. Trying to hold an umbrella up and fighting against the snow, maybe swaying as we walked, our feet became unstable and it was a job to see where we were going. We were joking about the state we were in and then heard this voice, 'Good Evening girls, see you in a minute'. It was the Rev Stally! If nothing brings you back to reality, that does, hearing the vicar at that time of night ordering you to church, knowing we had to appear the angelic choristers in the church choir in twenty minutes.

We did, however, manage it but unfortunately one of the other girls didn't and promptly passed out during 'The First Nowell'!

After the much loved Emrys Jones and his wife, it was during the 60s that the Rev Stally and his wife Anne had arrived in Alcester.

Mrs Stally opened up the big Rectory House as a children's pre-school nursery. Situated in the heart of the town, at the end of the High Street, the ideal place. So many happy years were spent there by the children. Each room was educational yet great fun. I well remember one room with a large ship placed in the corner, it was called The Captain's Cabin. This large nursery, like any other school, would have their open days providing an insight into what the children did during the morning and filling every parent with awe. The children were far too busy to see or even want their parents around. Milk and biscuits were brought to each room mid morning. The large garden was used in the summer as a play area and was all that any child could need for enjoyment.

By the time the children were old enough for 'proper' school they were well educated to cope with what was ahead for them. Mrs Stally had nurtured each and every one of the hundreds of children who passed through the door ready for 'big' school. I remember her telling me how my children would be as they grew up. She predicted right.

Christmas, again was very special for the children. Not only did they have a party but Father Christmas arrived with a gift, a Magician would turn up as entertainment, as they all sat round the Christmas tree in the lounge. Just like today, The Nativity scene was acted out in St Nicholas Church which was the highlight for the end of the year.

The Rev Arthur Stally threw himself into many activities not only in the church, but within the community. In one such 'family' service he decided to use a sheep in his talk to the families. There we were sat in the choir stalls, hearing a scuffling noise coming from the vestry. Out came the Rector with this sheep! Like many of his talks, it proved to go down very well.

The Rector was very much into Steam Engines. There was a special event one summer in the 60s at Kings Coughton and he wanted volunteers to clean and polish this engine up ready for the event. A handful of us set to and spent all morning making the engine gleam with pride outside the Rectory House. Another year a Donkey Derby was held at Ragley Hall. Yes, the Rev Stally was seen as one of the contestants on a donkey aiming to win.

The church grounds had become a little sad with no flowers to welcome people. Len Chambers did his best to keep everything spick and span but St Nicholas church gardens are a very large area so a group of people decided to give it some attention.

During this time I had been seeing, or courting, Eric Payne every night for four years. We had looked around to buy a house but everyone was gazumping us at the time. On walking into church one Sunday evening, Reverend Arthur Stally greeted us with, 'when are you two getting married? I have these marriage leaflets here but I see no point in giving you two one, just sort yourselves out and come to me with a wedding date'. This was at the beginning of October. We explained that we couldn't find a house, to which he replied, 'there's one waiting for you in School Road'. We were amazed but he explained that the house hadn't been lived in for some time, it was an old clergy house and needed a good refurbishment before it was inhabitable. That same evening we went to see it. Of course there was no electricity, but we just felt that this was the house. It was very obvious that a vast amount wanted attention. However, my two brothers Stan and David took over, banned us from the house and transformed it by the end of November. We were married December 6th, 1972 and moved straight in.

Here we see Marian Trout, Winnie Biddle and Eric Payne tidying up the small entrance to the church. Three very dedicated people who were there every evening, planting weeding and watering.

We soon found that the children at the school, right next door, realised they had neighbours next to the playground. They would reach up to the windows and wave to us as we sat on the sofa. Always followed by the clapping of the teachers hand shouting 'GET AWAY FROM THOSE WINDOWS!' It didn't help as we would wave back to them.

Elections were held at the school at this time, so each time it occurred, I would make cakes and coffee and be the 'runner' for refreshments for those working on the Election Day.

School House where we lived when first married.

ALCESTER 'MOP' FAIR

The first sign of autumn came when nights grew dark and the weather changed just as the Annual 'Mop' fair arrived. The Court Leet held a function annually in the ancient Town Hall. Afterwards the top window would open and the High Bailiff would throw pennies out to the children, eagerly waiting to catch them. The fairground normally came to town in damp drizzly weather. Locals had a saying for this kind of weather, "It's 'puthery' again. A sign the Mop has come to town".

In the 50s and 60s the mop was something to behold. As soon as the summer had gone families would save their money ready for the Mop. Children would have a free ticket given to them at school to ride on their favourite carousel.

The travelling families from the Mop would arrive late Sunday afternoon and park their caravans in the narrow road called Malt Mill Lane, or down the old Stratford Road by the football field. I would stay at my friend's house over night, she lived in the lane where the caravan homes would be. We would lean out of her tiny bedroom window and see the sparkling ornaments and lights in the caravans. Another world! How quickly they worked to get all the stalls and rides up.

Immediately outside the church were the Ginny Horses, run by Mr Bill Brewer, always remembered for his handlebar moustache and hook as a hand! As a young man of 18, his father owned a large set of steam driven galloping horses, which they were selling. They prepared it ready for inspection and were waiting for the steam to get up to full pressure. Whilst they were waiting, Bill climbed to the top of the machinery to make sure that everything was well greased. The man who was buying the ride arrived and the steam was now up to full power, so they started the ride to show it in full working order, not realising that Bill was still at the top of the ride and his hand was cut clean off by the moving machinery. Old Billy Brewer had a very ornate hand-turned juvenile, which had horses and vintage cars on at Alcester Mop by the church gate. Everyone remembers him because of his hook hand. His wife, Mrs Brewer would always visit Buntings shop to buy loads of Danish bacon.

There was a caravan, always a picture to see, with Gypsy Rose Lee sat inside. It was the only time I ever saw my mother have her fortune told.

On the 'Hook a Duck' stall would be the deaf and dumb lady. She had a way of reaching out to you, always with a smile.

Every year the highlight of going to school was to get your free ticket to go on the traditional Mop Fair. I still wonder why the craze was to wear cowboy hats when visiting the Mop, the trend seemed to last for years.

THE LEGENDARY PAT WHEELER

Alcester was blessed with a gentleman called Patrick Wheeler. Mr Wheeler, not only controlled the youth of the town but was MC at the local dances, mentioned before. He was a solicitor and could be seen walking through the town in a black pin striped suit and waistcoat, bowler hat and carrying a stick. A very distinguished man.

Alcester Cadets.

Alcester Cadets reunion.

Here was a gentleman who took the Alcester boys in hand. He formed the Alcester Cadets and instructed many Alcester boys. Three times a week they had instruction, drill and paraded from a hut in Stratford Road to the Grammar School. Each played an instrument, usually the bugle or drums. Barry Green was Drum Major, Robert Green followed on, while John Wright played the bass drum. How we need a Pat Wheeler today.

As children we would run through Alcester to walk alongside them until they reached the Grammar School where no one was allowed to follow. This group of boys went on to win many tournaments for the town.

In the years that followed those boys would always call him 'Sir' even as grown adults and give Mr Patrick Wheeler the greatest respect. No way would you backchat this gentleman or certainly let him down by getting into trouble. He was an honourable leader – a legend. It was heart warming to see so many 'old boys' turn up at his funeral.

In later years the cadets decided to have a reunion which proved a great success, raising a glass to Mr Patrick Wheeler.

CARNIVALS

It seemed to be an annual tradition every summer, that many organisations would take part in the Carnival. The very first (before my time) was a group of people, forming a Band! Commonly known as The Zicky Davis Tramp Band, so I am told. Many years later another 'band' was formed for the Carnival, Billy's Ragtime Band.

Each year after, the task began in finding a lorry, getting up early in the morning to decorate it and then enjoying the rocky drive through the town. One particular year a group of us from the Alcester Drama Group decided to be Hawaiian girls dressed in nothing else but grass skirts and a flowered bra bought from Woolworths and swaying to the music, propped up in the corner of the lorry. We did so well winning 1st prize and then going on to Bidford and Redditch doing the same thing.

The Zicky Davis Tramp Band.

Another year the same group decided to do Robin Hood and his Merry Men. How stupid was that! We covered the lorry with greenery which obviously by lunchtime was wilting!!! Needless to say we did not win anything.

Several years later the staff from Buntings shop were told that the theme was going to be pantomimes that year, so we decided to do Cinderella. What a great time we had!

The Lorries would leave from one end of the town and drive to the Greig Memorial Hall where an afternoon fete took place, with the Town Band playing all afternoon, along with many side shows and other entertainment.

Alcester Carnival float. 'Cinderella' with the author as Prince Charming on the right.

A FEW LITTLE ESCAPADES!

It was in the 60s that I left school and found a new world of freedom. I began to take liberties at home. I was encouraged by the local Drama group to go for a drink after the last performance of our pantomimes. I told my mother there was a party after in the Greig Memorial Hall. This was a small fib! My friend and I travelled with the boys in an Austin 1100 (sometimes six or seven in the car) to the Three Witches Pub at Stratford. I was late getting home and I had 'borrowed' the key on the promise it would be given back next morning.

Whatever time we returned home I don't remember but next morning at breakfast, my mother asked me how the party went, I said 'Oh it was fine'. She then said 'Did you take your suitcase upstairs with your costumes in before you went to bed?' I replied 'Yes'. Here is when she caught me out! Apparently I was dropped off quickly at my house; Mick Malin and co. had thrown my case over the hedge where it was looking at us both in the front garden next morning! I never did give the key back, always making an excuse I couldn't find it. My mother would say I was worse than all my six older brothers put together in my late teens!

All my brothers were different. Being as I was eight years younger than my brother Phillip, and 21 years younger than my brother Gordon, life seemed pretty strange as no doubt my mother didn't quite know how to handle a girl!

Stanley, next in line was the local builder with my father. He continued his profession for many years until he retired. My father and he would arrive home at 5 o'clock in the green lorry when I was promptly told to go in the other room! I think I got on their nerves chattering!

Gordon, the eldest was married when I was about 4 years old, but sadly I do not remember it. Gordon called weekly as he lived away. I knew he ran a club called 'Littlewoods' where my mother would occasionally purchase bed linen. One evening Gordon knocked on the door, I opened it and shouted to my mother, 'Mom… it's the club man' to which I was promptly told it was my brother! How was I to know?!

Michael, I will always remember for ringing me up on the telephone proclaiming he was Father Christmas. I really believed him, not realising he was my brother!

Norman always had time for me to dance in the living room, rocking and rolling, throwing me over his shoulder and taking me for rides in his old car.

David was affectionately named the 'Duke'. He had to be spotless before he went out in the evening. No one could get in the bathroom until he came out.

Phillip? We were always sparring partners. He would get me into trouble and vice versa, but nothing too nasty. As our neighbours next door had a television and we didn't, my brother and I would go there and watch TV. He with his mate Bobby and me with my friend Maureen. At 9 o'clock my mother would get the poker and bang on the wall for me to go home. I always dragged it out until the third bang on the wall. As I was getting up to leave Phillip lit a cigarette up. I was shocked and he could tell! He offered me half a crown not to tell my mother. However, on going home my mother said 'was Phillip still next door?' What did I do? Only say yes he's with Bobby Locke smoking his head off. After that I ran upstairs knowing I had caused big trouble. Some sister I was!

Now I am nearing the end of some of the escapades as the 60s were something else. The dangerous age when boys and men were plentiful! Of course I'm not going to go through them all, like most people we all went through joy and pain and many adventures, some good, some bad, but all part of life's rich tapestry.

Suffice to say, when I met Eric Payne and the marriage was to be announced, my mother had been in my bedroom previously!!! She advised me to get rid of a list I had kept of different boyfriends I had seen over the years. I would put a tick by the nice ones and a cross by the not so nice!

Her last words to Eric (who would be my husband) were 'I wish you well Eric; I hope you know what you are taking on. You have my blessing'!

Arrangements were made, but the hardest thing I had to choose was who to have as attendants. In the end as we both had so many nieces and nephews, the thought suddenly dawned on us! Who was the one person I was closest to, who I shared everything with together, never arguing about trivial things? It had to be my good friend Esme.

Wedding day.

We were married in December by the Rev Arthur Stally. At least the tradition still goes on that many locals like to wait at the gates of the church to see the bride and her entourage go in. It was a beautiful service with a reception afterwards at the Hannah Susan Greig Memorial Hall for 140 people.

As everyone was gathered, I couldn't find my bridesmaid. After searching the building in the distance I saw Esme walking to meet us. Apparently I had forgotten to book a car for the poor girl!

Not long after a document was posted through the letter box 'demanding' that we go to Alcester Town Hall for a Court appearance!!! After reading it through three times we realised that after many years someone in their wisdom had nominated us and two more couples for the Ancient Tradition called The Flitch.

You have to be cross-examined by a gentleman who was counsel for the Flitch. None other than Mr Pat Wheeler. My goodness they had done their homework in secret! We, as with the others had to convince the court we had been married a year but one day.

Alcester Town Hall.

We were told to wait downstairs while Sergeant John Searson stood in front of the double doors. The first couple were called, we could hear murmurs, then laughter but no idea what was going on.

It came to our turn and Sergeant Searson, before opening the doors, said 'Be warned, there are no seats left, the audience are on the stairs also'. There was no time to think! Up we got in the box and swore we would tell the truth, the whole truth all but a day.

Oh my goodness, where did they find out what we had been doing and who we had been seeing during the year? For example:

Our Flitch trial.

'Why are your husband and your bridesmaid always late going into church?' My reply was because they are both bell ringers and have to finish ringing before they come to the service.

'Can you explain why you were seen kissing the vicar?' My reply was because I was very grateful for all he had done for us.

These were just two examples but sadly, as the dumb blonde that I am, words came out wrong many times to which the audience were crying with laughter. Needless to say we won the side of bacon which is the tradition for the winner.

As I worked at the local grocer and delicatessen I was able to have everything cut and sliced up for me. We gave it all to the many people who we couldn't ask to the wedding and ended up with the bits left over for ourselves. Very shortly after that our son was born, followed three years later by our daughter.

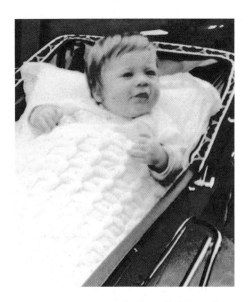 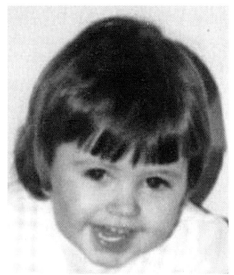

Left: first child Nick. Right: second child Charlie.

This is my Alcester as I remember it. Over the years, life changes we all go into another episode of our life. We all keep those memories. Variety was, and is the spice of life. Long may it continue, in now a far more modern age.